What's New in The New NHS?

a handbook for the pharmaceutical industry

by
Paul Barnett

Foreword by
Professor David Taylor

Editor
Joanna Lyford

BROOKWOOD MEDICAL PUBLICATIONS

About the Author

Paul Barnett's career with the Department of Health covered most aspects of Government and NHS policies on the management of medicines in the NHS. He was a member of the Prescribing Branch where he took part in the development and implementation of the Selected List of NHS Drugs working for the then Minister for Health, Kenneth Clarke. He also worked with Health Authorities and the Department's Regional Medical Officers on prescribing issues and with the Prescription Pricing Authority (PPA) in developing the prototype Prescribing And Cost Analyses (PACT) for GPs and Health Authorities.

He also worked with the PPA when in the Department's Information Management Group in developing the Indicative Prescribing system. He was in charge of the GP practice computerisation programme, at a time when the percentage of computerised practices rose from less that 25% to 85% in five years. He also worked with community pharmacists on the development of their systems and with GPs, community pharmacists and the PPA on early trial electronic prescription links.

Later, he was a member of the Department's Pharmaceutical Industry branch where he negotiated with pharmaceutical companies on their annual profits on sales of medicines to the NHS under the Pharmaceutical Price Regulation Scheme (PPRS). During this period he also worked with the Medicines Control Agency, the NHS Supplies Authority, the Home Office on the legal use of controlled drugs in the NHS, the Department of Trade & Industry on related trade issues and the Department of the Environment on the Pharmaceutical Industry related issues on the European Community directive on packaging.

He contributed to the development of the joint Government/Industry 'Prescribe UK' inward investment initiative in respect of potential investment from the Japanese industry. He was one of the UK representatives on the Brussels-based EU Pharmaceutical Pricing

Transparency Committee, the main forum for discussing EU-wide issues on pharmaceuticals and the Pharmaceutical Industry. Throughout this time he worked with his opposite numbers in Scotland, Wales and Northern Ireland.

Since leaving the Department of Health to set up his own consultancy, he has earned a reputation with pharmaceutical companies for providing concise and focused briefings on key Government and NHS issues.

Contents

Foreword

by Professor David Taylor

When Tony Blair's administration came to power in 1997 its approach
to health policy and the future of the NHS was strong on criticism of
the previous government, but weak on what the new government was
going to do to improve health and health care. The harm and inequity
that Tory innovations such as GP fundholding were said to have
created would be stopped by the elimination of the NHS internal
market. Yet what would follow in its place to ensure ongoing progress
was uncertain.

Two years later the situation is much clearer. Labour's policies to take
the NHS into the new millennium in fact build logically on the health
sector changes in England and other parts of the UK achieved during
the 1980s and 1990s. GP fundholding has been terminated; the
rhetoric of the health care market has also gone. However, the
commissioner/provider divide within the NHS lives on, as does the
aim of introducing not only more rigorous – centrally accountable –
health care quality management, but also a 'primary care led' service.
Reports of the demise of GP budget holding and the associated loss
of family practitioner power have been premature, and exaggerated.

Pharmaceutical Industry impact

The three main pillars supporting New Labour's New NHS are:

- *Creation of Primary Care Groups and Trusts*
  These will in time promote the development of more
  corporate approaches to the local delivery of primary care,
  involving all professionals rather than just those in more
  forward looking practices. Unified budgets should also
  drive more flexible and efficient resource use, even if at
  first a 'silo budgeting' mentality prevails.
- *Development of a more integrated approach to quality*
  The creation of the National Institute for Clinical
  Excellence opens the way to more consistent standard

5

setting in England and Wales; clinical governance systems should facilitate better delivery; and the work of the Commission for Health Improvement will contribute to better monitoring of health service provision, and the control and correction of quality problems.

- *New public health*

   The breakdown of what Frank Dobson has termed the 'Berlin Wall' between health and social care coupled with more informed approaches to promoting better health though environmental, dietary and behavioural changes, will augment – and in some important instances outweigh – the health gains to be derived from better medical treatments.

The policies and programmes emerging in these fields have important implications for the Pharmaceutical Industry, both in the UK and internationally. They promise significant shifts in the way the value of medicines is assessed, and the processes by which they are provided to patients. When seen in the light of events such as the renegotiation of the PPRS and the passage of the Health Bill through Parliament, their potential impact is profound. The UK could well set a precedent which will influence other markets across Europe, and the rest of the world.

Understanding a changing environment

Against this background, Paul Barnett's handbook represents a valuable resource for people in all industries serving the health service, as well as to managers and professionals directly employed in the public sector. It contains timely summaries of many important policy initiatives, and current approaches to their implementation.

His analyses of issues and topics ranging from the formation of Primary Care Groups/Trusts and the establishment of National Service Frameworks to Health Action Zones, the significance of social exclusion in the New Labour policy climate, and prescribing incentive and support programmes will be useful to senior executives and junior researchers alike. It offers keys to unlocking not only sales opportunities, but also the challenge of establishing stronger partnerships between public and private service organisations.

Effective marketing

As the twenty-first century progresses, enhanced understandings in the biomedical sciences will open up many new therapeutic options. If used as fully as possible to satisfy patient needs and improve consumers' lives, they will have the potential to earn innovators returns on today's investments, and provide the resources and confidence needed to support further research. Yet the successful marketing of any new treatment depends not only on its inherent properties, but also the successful communication of its possible benefits to those who will prescribe it, pay for it, and consume it.

Seen in this light, producing new medicines alone will never be enough to ensure patient well-being or commercial success. Achieving these goals also demands a sensitive awareness of the needs of customers at all levels of the health care supply chain. The latter include Ministers under pressure from the Treasury, NHS managers torn between central imperstives and locally expressed demands, and NHS staff striving to help individual patients cope with the complex challenges of life despite the sometimes unhelpful restrictions and regulations imposed upon them.

Paul Barnett's meticulous work – based on his long experience within the Department of Health – goes a considerable way to meeting this need, and so enables the providers of medicines and other vital products and services to talk the language of those responsible for their purchase.

David Taylor is Director of Health Affairs at GJW Government Relations and visiting Professor of Health and Medicines Policy at the School of Pharmacy, University of London. He is also an external Professor of the Welsh Institute for Health and Social Care. Professor Taylor has chaired an NHS Authority and served as an Associate Director of the Audit Commission. He was Director of Public and Economic Affairs at the ABPI between 1983 and 1989.

Introduction

What's it all about?

From 1999, the current 'internal market' arrangements in the NHS for GP fundholders and GP Commissioning Groups are being replaced with Primary Care Groups.

Previously about 60% of the patient population was covered by GP fundholding practices. These practices managed their own budgets and were able to commission care for their patients by referral to hospital Trusts. The remaining GP practices had care for their patients commissioned on their behalf by their Health Authorities on advice from commissioning groups representing the practices. This was criticised for encouraging a two-tier system, whereby patients from fundholding practices received priority treatment from Trusts because the money for their treatment came directly from the practices. When the present Government came to power, it immediately put a stop to preferential treatment for GP fundholder patients and proposed putting all GP practices on an equal footing by bringing them together in Primary Care Groups (PCGs).

Each PCG will consist of around 50 GPs and nurses and cover around 100,000 patients. PCGs can take on different degrees of responsibility, from advising Health Authorities (HAs) on commissioning decisions to acting as free-standing Primary Care Trusts. The former is likely to appeal to GPs who have not yet been involved in either fundholding or commissioning. The latter is more likely to appeal to GPs who are due to lose their fundholding status. It expected that Primary Care Trusts will assume responsibility for community health services currently run by Community Health Trusts.

PCGs will work with HAs in commissioning services from Trusts as well as managing their own cash-limited budgets. The budgets are unified covering funds for hospital and community services, general medical services and prescribing. For the first time, GPs will be able to transfer between the funds (i.e. both into and out of the prescribing budgets) according to what they see as the most clinical and cost effective treatment for patients. It will also be possible to transfer funds from hospital and community health and Local Authority social services budgets into PCG budgets where there is agreement by all concerned that this is the preferred 'pathway of care'. This is in tune with the new Health Action Zones and other public health measures to rectify inequalities of health and health care.

PCGs will work with HAs, Trusts and Local Authorities to develop Health Improvement Programmes, i.e. to identify local health needs and develop the services accordingly. These will cover a three year period. There is to be a statutory responsibility on HAs and LAs to work together to produce Joint Investment Plans.

Local planning will take place within a national framework set by the Government. The NHS Executive (NHSE) will continue to define national priorities for the NHS as set out in *Our Healthier Nation*. They will also set National Service Frameworks, which aim to bring together the best evidence of clinical and cost-effectiveness to determine the best ways of providing particular services. To ensure consistent access to beneficial care across the NHS, the National Institute for Clinical Excellence (NICE) will develop clinical guidelines based on current evidence of clinical and cost-effectiveness. NICE will cover drugs as well as other forms of treatment.

To ensure the success of national guidelines and local planning, the new Commission for Health Improvement will support and oversee the improvement of quality in clinical care, and will have inspectorate powers. In addition there will be a new National Performance Framework to assess the performance of health care providers with an emphasis on measurable health outcomes. There will also be a National Schedule of Reference Costs, against which local costs of delivering care will be 'benchmarked' against national average costs.

All Chief Executives in the NHS will have a statutory responsibility for clinical governance (i.e. the quality of care provided) which will extend to all clinicians and other health professionals.

Government powers to manage the introduction of new medicines in the NHS are to be strengthened by the use of the Selected List of Drugs regulations. The list will restrict availability to specified patients and/or conditions and through new statutory powers will limit the price and/or pharmaceutical company profits from sales to the NHS.

Importance to the Pharmaceutical Industry

Business Managers will need to identify who within the PCGs is likely to be making the key prescribing decisions, and monitor the extent to which PCG-based formularies replace those currently drawn up by individual practices or HAs. They will want to target key prescribers within the PCG to ensure that the case for the Company's products is properly represented in terms of clinical and cost- effectiveness. There is likely to be a renewed drive to reduce inequities in generic prescribing, which currently accounts for 50-70% of all prescriptions. They will also want to be aware of developments affecting prescribing in pilot trials starting in their area in 1998. Under the new arrangements, GPs will remain independent contractors with the right to make their own prescribing decisions. The Government has also given the commitment in the White Paper that "all patients will have proper access to the medicines they require". Although cash-limited, the PCG budgets allow cash to be transferred into the prescribing part of the budget where necessary.

Product Managers will want to ensure that the national service frameworks and clinical guidelines drawn up by NHSE and NICE fairly reflect the value of their products in clinical and cost-effectiveness terms. They will also want to be assured that PCGs, HAs and Trusts take proper account of these frameworks and guidelines when drawing up local health improvement programmes and any associated recommendations on prescribing. They will need to see how the Government's clinical effectiveness and other indicators may help or hinder the future sales. The outcome of investigations by the Commission for Health Improvement using the criteria set for the national performance framework may be helpful in monitoring activity.

The Boards of Management will want to assess the net impact of the changes on their product range. They will want to identify which of their products are likely to be at risk and which are likely to prosper, given the Government's choice of priorities for the NHS. They need to build a solid working relationship with NICE, and ensure that their products, if selected for appraisal, get a fair hearing. They will try to ensure that the period of uncertainty whilst the product is being appraised is minimised, and that the appraisal results in consistency in decision-making across the NHS. They will also want to assess the potential impact of the Selected List of Drugs and the new powers to limit prices and profits on their future business. They will need to assess what impact this will have on their view of the Pharmaceutical Price Regulation Scheme.

Setting national priorities

What's it all about?
Our Healthier Nation, the Government's Green Paper on Public Health, aims to establish a 'contract of health' with the nation which will improve the health of the population as a whole. This will be achieved by increasing the length of people's lives and the number of years spent free of illness, and by improving the health of the worst off in society.

Four target areas have been identified: cancer, chronic heart disease and stroke, accidents and mental health. These will account for around 75% of all deaths each year.

Guidelines on national priorities for the health and social services for 1999-2002, which Health Authorities (HAs) and Local Authorities (LAs) are expected to incorporate into their local Health Improvement Programmes (HImPs) for 1999 onwards, support the aims of the Green Paper. This is the first time that health and social services priorities have been issued jointly and the first time that they have covered a three year period. This is line with Government proposals to make HAs and LAs jointly accountable for services and for long-term service agreements.

Key points
- national priorities will be led either by the NHS, or by social services, or jointly by the two bodies
- jointly-led priorities include cutting health inequalities (e.g. reducing the rate of unwanted teenage pregnancies), reduction of accidents (e.g. fractures amongst the elderly through osteoporosis) and reducing social isolation (e.g. mentally ill)
- NHS-led priorities include improving the cost and clinical effectiveness of prescribing, including more generic prescribing and improving the early detection and treatment of cancer and chronic heart disease
- all priorities are linked to key policy documents (e.g. the targets in *Our Healthier Nation*, the measures for improving prescribing in the *GP Prescribing Support* resource documents)
- targets to meet the priorities are expected to be incorporated in HImPs
- the Commission for Health Improvement will monitor their implementation

Importance to the Pharmaceutical Industry

The relevance of the national priorities to the Pharmaceutical Industry are more obvious in certain instances, e.g. oral contraceptives and teenage pregnancies, the role of drug treatment in chronic heart disease, HRT and the reduction of fractures through osteoporosis. Much of the Government's strategy is underpinned by a commitment to the screening and early detection of illness, which has significant implications for diagnostics. Other national priorities may be of less obvious interest, but nevertheless medicines still play a significant role (e.g. in reducing waiting lists by reducing the need for avoidable hospital admissions, reducing social exclusion of patients with long-term medical conditions and the mentally ill).

Given the strong 'policing' of the inclusion of national priorities in HImPs, the monitoring of their implementation by the Commission for Health Improvement (CHI) and the likely use of the national priorities for prioritising the allocation of resources by HAs, it is important that the relevance of products to the priorities is made explicit.

Quality in the New NHS

What's it all about?
A First Class Service is the Government document on quality issues in the NHS. It covers National Service Frameworks (NSFs), clinical governance, the National Institute for Clinical Excellence (NICE) and the Commission for Health Improvement (CHI).

Key points
- NSFs to set national standards and define service models
- NICE to provide advice to NSFs on best practice for existing treatments and appraise new interventions
- Horizon Scanning Centre to identify significant new interventions well in advance of expected NHS launch
- all NHS organisations to be accountable for quality of service through clinical governance
- CHI to use NSFs and performance indicators to assess prescribing and other performance of clinicians

Importance to the Pharmaceutical Industry
The Pharmaceutical Industry will be expected to provide NICE with evidence of clinical and cost-effectiveness in support of new and existing products, and to collaborate with the Health and Safety Commission (HSC) well in advance of any new product launch. Failure to do so may lead to restrictions on use within the NHS.

Clinicians retain the right of clinical freedom to prescribe what they consider best for their patients, but will come under increasing pressure to conform with NSFs where they exist. NICE prescribing recommendations will be included in the Prodigy decision support systems used by GPs. CHI is likely to critically examine any clinician who consistently strays from the norm.

The practical implications of these changes remain to be seen. The ethical and legal issues concerning the refusal of treatment for patients who may benefit from it have yet to be addressed. However, companies which are able to demonstrate clinical and cost-effectiveness of products stand to gain, especially if there is support for them in NSFs and local Health Improvement Programmes.

Clinical governance

What's it all about?
From April 1999 Acute and Community Trusts, and in due course Primary Care Groups, will have a statutory responsibility for setting and meeting quality standards of care (including the appropriate and efficient use of medicines). Failure to meet these standards could make them liable to challenge in the Courts.

Key points
- performance of clinicians, other health professionals and NHS managers in providing services will be assessed
- efficient use of resources (including medicines) will be judged
- risk of injury or illness associated with the service provided (including medicines) will be assessed
- patients' satisfaction with services will be taken on board
- the Commission for Health Improvement will assess the performance of Trusts, and in due course Primary Care Groups, every 3-4 years

Importance to the Pharmaceutical Industry
The problem with the proposals for clinical governance is not what they say, but what they mean. Local and national responsibilities for quality of care are yet to be defined.

Medicines have an advantage over most other interventions in that to become licensed they have already passed a basic test of safety and efficacy. However, clinical governance will add to the pressure on prescribers to conform with the accepted norm, since to do otherwise may leave them open to legal liability. In the end, a clinician's right to prescribe a particular medicine not recommended by the National Institute for Clinical Excellence (for example) may have to be resolved in the Courts. The current legal principle of the right to deviate from accepted medical practice where the clinical choice is seen as reasonable given the individual circumstances of the patient (the 'Bolam Test') may be challenged in the light of new legislation passed to implement clinical governance.

National Service Frameworks

What's it all about?
National Service Frameworks (NSFs) set national standards and models of service for selected services or care groups. They include strategies for implementation and performance measures by which HAs, PCGs and Trusts will assessed by the CHI.

Key points
- selection of NSFs primarily determined by national targets and priorities set in *Our Healthier Nation*
- first NSFs (1998/99) will be on chronic heart disease and mental health
- subsequently one NSF will be developed per annum according to set criteria
- the current cancer service framework (Calman/Hine) is seen as one of the models for future NSFs
- NSFs will include an assessment of health and social care needs, service configuration guidance, clinical guidelines and evidence on effective and efficient interventions and organisational arrangements
- assessment of medicines and other interventions by NICE will be a key element
- development of each NSF will be assisted by an expert reference group including clinical professionals, NHS managers, patients and carers representatives and industry
- NSFs signal tighter central control and may be used by

HAs to justify rationing decisions
- will be used by the CHI in assessing clinicians and NHS managers' performance
- balance between NSFs and Government's commitment to meeting local health need (via Health Improvement Programmes) not yet clear

Importance to the Pharmaceutical Industry

NSFs will implement the Government's agenda as set out in *Our Healthier Nation*. Companies with products in priority areas – cancer, chronic heart disease, accidents and mental health – will benefit most. Companies with products outside areas defined by NSF may find that HAs use them to justify restriction of choices (including advice on prescribing) to what is covered by the NSF. The Pharmaceutical Industry might like to consider the scope for lobbying for NSFs which carry positive messages about the appropriate use of medicines (e.g. on reducing unwanted teenage pregnancies, asthma prevention and treatment for children).

Where NSFs are being developed, they are supported by expert reference groups which may include Industry representatives and focus on examples of good practice. Where appropriate, the Pharmaceutical Industry may like to consider membership of a reference group and/or what the company might be able to contribute by example towards the development of the NSF.

National Institute for Clinical Excellence

The National Institute for Clinical Excellence (NICE) assesses new and current medicines, interventions and services used in the NHS.

Key points
- NICE to assess 30-50 significant new and existing clinical interventions each year, of which 90% are likely to be medicines in the first year
- newly-established Partner's Council with patient and

Industry representation will appraise new clinical interventions
- NICE will replace all other bodies assessing medicines (except the Medicines Control Agency) to avoid duplication and ensure consistency
- NICE to publish annual National Survey of Patient and User Experience
- the National Prescribing Centre and responsibility for Prodigy prescribing guidelines to be absorbed by NICE
- selection of interventions for assessment will be made well in advance of NHS launch
- pharmaceutical companies expected to provide evidence of clinical and cost effectiveness of products to NICE
- threat of stronger powers for NICE and CHI if HAs/ Trusts/PCGs/clinicians and the Industry do not co-operate

Importance to the Pharmaceutical Industry

The Pharmaceutical Industry will be expected to provide NICE with evidence of clinical and cost-effectiveness in support of new and existing products and to collaborate well in advance of any new product launch. Failure to do so may lead to restrictions on use in the NHS. The Government has also signalled that it is prepared to use its statutory powers to restrict prescribing and fix prices if the Industry does not co-operate.

Clinicians retain the right of clinical freedom to prescribe what they consider best for their patients, but will come under increasing pressure to conform with NICE. NICE prescribing recommendations will be included in the Prodigy decision support systems used by GPs. CHI are likely to examine critically any clinician who consistently strays from the norm.

What this means in practice remains to be seen. The ethical and legal issues concerning the refusal of treatment for patients who may benefit from it have yet to be addressed. However, companies which are able to demonstrate clinical and cost effectiveness of products stand to gain most.

The Pharmaceutical Industry will need to ensure that there is level playing field when it comes to assessing medicines against alternative interventions.

Commission for Health Improvement

What's it all about?
The Commission for Health Improvement (CHI) will regularly assess the performance of Trusts, Health Authorities (HAs) and Primary Care Groups (PCGs) in meeting national and local standards of quality of care, including the prescribing of medicines.

Key points
- CHI to visit each acute, community and primary care Trust every 3-4 years
- CHI will also visit HAs and PCGs which are not Trusts if what they are doing impacts on the work of the Trusts (e.g. the prescribing of medicines)
- CHI will use National Institute for Clinical Excellence (NICE) guidelines, National Service Frameworks (NSFs), the National Framework for Assessing Performance (NFAP) and the National Schedule of Reference Costs in reviewing performance (all are likely to refer to medicines prescribed)
- CHI will conduct annual National Surveys of Patient and User Experiences which will enable comparisons of the service received (e.g. what medicines are prescribed) to be made at local level; output from NHS complaints procedures will also be used
- CHI will also conduct sample studies across the NHS to monitor progress on the implementation of NSFs and NICE guidance

Importance to the Pharmaceutical Industry
CHI will encourage prescribers to conform to national guidelines on prescribing. CHI will be reviewing the performance of clinicians

against NSFs, NICE guidelines and performance indicators in the National Framework for Assessing Performance. All will have recommendations on prescribing. Those pharmaceutical companies that have positive recommendations on medicines are likely to do best.

National Framework for Assessing Performance

What's it all about?
The Commission for Health Improvement will use a National Framework for Assessing Performance in assessing the performance (including the management of medicines) of HAs and Trusts in the NHS. The Framework includes prescribing indicators.

Key points
- covers six aspects of performance: health improvement, fair access to services, effective delivery of appropriate health care, efficiency, patient/carer experience and health outcomes of NHS care
- covers all the NHS (i.e. HAs, Trusts and PCGs)
- performance can be assessed by population group (e.g. the elderly, children), by disease area (e.g. asthma, osteoporosis, chronic heart disease, cancer), by HA, Trust or PCG or by service/service sector (e.g. diagnostics, primary care or mental health)
- indicators of performance include clinical effectiveness based on research evidence, cost per unit of care/outcome, responsiveness to individual needs and preferences, patient involvement, good information and choice, reduced levels of risk, reduced levels of disease, impairment and complications of treatment, improved quality of life for patients and carers, and reduced premature deaths

Importance to the Pharmaceutical Industry
The Framework will be used to assess how well medicines are being managed in the NHS. Pharmaceuticals companies need to assess how

well their products are likely to perform within the parameters set by the Framework. The outcome of the Framework's indicators may be helpful in identifying where, in the Government's opinion, certain HAs could improve their performance and achieve appropriate levels of prescribing (e.g. higher levels of HRT).

Clinical effectiveness indicators

What's it all about?
Clinical effectiveness indicators will be used to compare the effectiveness of a particular service provided by different HAs. They will be one of the tools used in the National Framework for Assessing Performance for measuring the performance individuals and organisations in the NHS. The pilot indicators, and those likely to follow, can be used to measure the relative effectiveness of medicines compared with other forms of treatment.

Key points
- there are 14 pilot clinical effectiveness indicators including those for treating cancer, menorrhagia and chronic heart disease and include, where appropriate, medicines
- they are aimed at areas with unmet needs and a higher rate of use than desirable (e.g. HRT, statins); where the intervention is inappropriate and a decrease in use would be desirable (e.g. benzodiazepines); or where there is marked variation is use between HAs and it is unclear whether there should be more or less use (e.g. surgical vs medical management of heart disease)
- they are one of a set of indicators included in the National Framework for Assessing Performance
- they will be used by patients and their representatives, the NHS Executive and the new Commission for Health Improvement for assessing HA/PCG/Trust performance

Importance to the Pharmaceutical Industry

The indicators will be used to assess the performance of HAs, Trusts and PCGs, including the effective use of medicines (e.g. the impact of effective use of hormone replacement therapy on the rate of hysterectomies). They pull together statistical data, policy aspirations and references to research and professional literature (e.g. the *BMJ*) into a single document. Assessments by NICE will be included in due course.

The Pharmaceutical Industry will need to ensure that company representatives at national and local level are aware of the indicators as they are likely to be referred to in discussions at all levels in the NHS. Secondly, the Industry may find the content of the specifications for the indicators helpful in shaping supporting promotional material for products. The NHS will expect the sort of information that is contained in the indicators and those which follow them.

National Schedule of Reference Costs

What's it all about?

All Trusts are required to collect reference cost data on selected specialities, including respiratory disease, neurology and rheumatology, as part of the development of a National Schedule of Reference Costs. This will enable Trusts to compare their performance and help HAs and PCGs to make commissioning decisions. It is likely to support contract negotiations for medicines which are to be for a longer period (three years). It will also help the CHI to assess the performance of Trusts and others on a variety of issues, including medicine purchase and utilisation.

Key points
- for the first time data will be collected on medical as well as surgical specialities
- Trusts will have to select specialities from a list to make up at least 40% of the inpatient and day case activity in 1998/99

- all Trusts will collect data on respiratory medicine
- general medicine, endocrinology, dermatology, rheumatology, audiological medicine, infectious diseases, gastroenterology, cardiology, neurology, paediatrics and genitourinary medicine are also on the list
- Health Resource Group costings are to be used
- Trusts will have to supply reference costs for all medical specialities by 1999/2000

Importance to the Pharmaceutical Industry

The NHS Executive sees respiratory care as a priority target in comparing the performance of Trusts and others in the NHS (it is the only speciality for which costings are compulsory). The National Schedule of Reference Costs is likely to be a key tool in contract negotiations between Trusts and pharmaceutical companies on the supply of medicines, and between Trusts, HAs and PCGs on commissioning services and deciding where best to allocate resources.

Other factors such as the impact on total health costs, the quality of the service provided and greater flexibility on budgets should off-set decisions made purely on cost grounds. However, it emphasises the need for pharmaceutical companies to support any cost-effective claims with sound, and preferably independent evidence-based material.

Commissioning services in the New NHS

What's it all about?

Commissioning of hospital and community services will be carried out by HAs and some PCGs (i.e. those at Level 3 or 4). Commissioning will be based on 'pathways of care' across the NHS, which will include the prescribing of medicines.

Key points
- all service agreements will be for a minimum of three years

- they will be negotiated with Trusts (Acute, Community and Primary) by HAs on behalf of Level 1 and 2 PCGs and by Level 3 and 4 PCGs
- they will be based on shared 'pathways of care' for patients crossing primary, secondary and tertiary and community care boundaries
- they will take account of the Government's national priorities, National Service Frameworks, NICE guidelines (including those on medicines) and local priorities set out in Health Improvement Programmes
- the National Schedule of Reference Costs will be used in costing the agreements
- how the agreements are costed will be transparent
- specialised services (e.g. cystic fibrosis, neuroscience, HIV/AIDS, haemophilia, intestinal failure, bone marrow transplant, genetic services) can be negotiated at national, regional or sub-regional level

Importance to the Pharmaceutical Industry

This guidance is fundamental to how goods and services, including medicines, are to be purchased in the NHS in the future. The shared pathways of care will have a prescribing element based on NICE recommendations and will cross the boundaries of primary and secondary care.

There is a useful checklist provided by the NHSE which sets out the questions HAs and PCGs should consider when negotiating service contracts. This may be helpful to pharmaceutical marketing teams in aligning their marketing strategy with the key issues facing commissioners in the NHS.

The list of specialised services has been greatly expanded and reflects the experience of the NHS over the last few years in dealing with technically advanced and costly treatments. Pharmaceutical companies may like to consider negotiating contracts for such treatments at each level allowed by the guidance, i.e. PCG, HA, sub-regional consortiums of HAS/PCGs, regional and national.

Health Improvement Programmes

What's it all about?

Health Improvement Programmes (HImPs) are three-year rolling plans for the development of health services at local level. They will provide the basis for accountability agreements between HAs and PCGs and for service agreements between HAs/PCGs and Trusts, both of which may include specifications on the use of medicines. The HImPs are to be developed by HAs in consultation with PCGs, Trusts, LAs, patient and voluntary groups and other local interests (e.g. NHS staff representatives, local businesses).

Key points

- three-year rolling programmes
- based on local needs assessment, national priorities and local health inequalities
- lead by HAs, the development of HImPs involves wide consultation inside and outside the NHS, including patient groups
- they will form the basis of accountability agreements between HAs and PCGs
- they will form the basis of service agreements between HAS/PCGs and Trusts
- may specify the use of prescribing protocols, formularies and measures set out in the National Prescribing Centre's GP Prescribing Support guide
- implementation to be monitored by the CHI using performance indicators including those for prescribing

Importance to the Pharmaceutical Industry

HImPs are central to the Government strategy for NHS service planning from 1999 and represent the blending of national and local priorities in terms of need and the clinical and cost-effective delivery of healthcare. Through accountability and service agreements, they are likely to include measures for prescribing such as the use of formularies, target levels for generic and repeat prescribing, NICE guidelines and protocols. These will be tightly managed by the HAs and progress monitored by CHI.

In all cases, this may lead to higher levels of prescribing in areas covered by the national priorities (e.g. for cancer and cardiovascular medicines, HRT, diagnostics). In some areas, it may lead to higher levels of prescribing where the HA is significantly below average, i.e. where there is a health inequality (e.g. hysterectomies vs HRT). There is also scope for more effective prescribing of medicines for conditions not covered by the national priorities but for which there is a pressing local need (e.g. where there is a high level of unwanted teenage pregnancies, high incidence of asthma amongst children through pollution).

The process of developing HImPs is intended to be as open as possible. The Pharmaceutical Industry might like to consider what scope there is for targeting key HAs and what input the company might want to make at a local level, either directly or through the relevant patient representative groups.

Health Action Zones

What's it all about?
A key feature of the Government's health strategy is the designation of a small number of areas where the need to improve the health of the population is greatest. These areas of high need will be known as Health Action Zones (HAZs), and will get priority in the allocation of additional resources. Inner city areas are an obvious target, but the Government remains open-minded to proposals to support other areas of deprivation (e.g. remote rural areas). Each zone will have a catchment area which encompasses at least one HA; there is no upper limit for the population coverage of an HAZ, and a single zone may cover more than one HA.

Key points
- involves HAs and LAs in partnership with community groups, the voluntary sector and local businesses
- priority access to public sector and Private Finance Initiative (PFI), National Lottery and EU funding

- investment by partners does not necessarily have to be financial, but could include expertise and other forms of support
- the Government is prepared to relax national requirements to accommodate local needs where appropriate
- initial funding for three years

Importance to the Pharmaceutical Industry

HAZs are likely to be high profile both for funding and publicity. Support does not necessarily have to be financial. Pharmaceutical companies should offer expertise and experience as well as access to archives of relevant material.

Healthy initiatives

What's it all about?

The Government is encouraging HAs, LAs and local businesses to work together in promoting a healthier lifestyle as part of its strategy in preventing ill health and reducing social isolation. There are to be three initiatives of this type: healthy neighbourhoods, healthy schools and healthy workplaces.

Key points

- Government is looking to local businesses and employers to set a good example
- the healthy neighbourhoods initiative is aimed at improving the environment for the elderly and disabled (e.g. better street lighting, better access to buildings);
- the healthy schools initiative is aimed at better health education for school children (e.g. nutrition, sex education, better understanding of asthma)
- the healthy workplaces initiative is aimed at improving the health of employees (e.g. healthy canteen menus, better exercise facilities, etc.)
- low cost options to make a contribution (e.g. by using materials and/or expertise already available)

Importance to the Pharmaceutical Industry

The three initiatives provide an opportunity for the Pharmaceutical Industry to enhance their public image. The Government will be looking to industries in the health sector to set a good example in the healthy workplaces initiative. There may also be opportunities under the healthy schools initiatives (e.g. on sex education). Today's school children will be tomorrow's opinion formers: the Industry should not pass up the opportunity to promote a positive image of it's work.

Social exclusion

What's it all about?

Social exclusion is a shorthand label for what can happen when individuals or areas suffer from a combination of linked problems such as unemployment, poor skills, low incomes, poor housing, high crime, bad health and family breakdown. The Social Exclusion Unit, based at the Cabinet Office, takes the lead on long-term issues of social deprivation which cross the boundaries of two or more Government departments' remits.

Key points

- aims to improve understanding of the key characteristics of social exclusion, and impact on Government policies
- promotes solutions by encouraging co-operation, disseminating best practice, and where necessary, making recommendations for changes in policies, machinery or delivery mechanisms
- key indicators of social exclusion and how these can be tracked will monitor the effectiveness of Government policies in reducing social exclusion
- priority tasks include truancy and school exclusions, street living, worst estates, and unwanted teenage pregnancies
- ways to encourage and focus individual and business involvement in tackling social exclusion being sought

Importance to the Pharmaceutical Industry

The Pharmaceutical Industry needs to be aware of the wider implications of health policy on its business. Industry leaders should also remember that Government departments other than the Department of Health may have an involvement. One key issue being considered by the Social Exclusion Unit is that of unwanted teenage pregnancies (i.e. the implications across the board for health, social services, housing, education, social security and employment).

Primary Care Groups

What's it all about?

Primary Care Groups (PCGs) will be responsible for managing the primary care services in the NHS. Each of the 480 PCGs in England will consist of around 50 GPs and nurses and cover on average 100,000 patients (ranging from 50,000 to 220,000). PCGs have a choice of status (Levels 1-4) ranging from merely advising HAs on commissioning decisions to becoming free standing Primary Care Trusts (PCTs). PCGs will work with HAs in commissioning services from Trusts as well as managing their own cash-limited budgets. The budgets are unified covering funds for hospital and community services, general medical services and prescribing.

Key points

- GP practice membership of a PCG is compulsory
- all PCGs will be either Level 1 or 2 in 1999/2000
- at least 50% of PCGs in 1999/2000 will be Level 2
- to be Level 2, the PCG must manage at least 40% of its unified budget in the first year and 60% in the second
- Level 1 and 2 PCGs will be part of HAs (i.e. sub-committees)
- GPs will form the majority on PCG Boards
- there will be representatives from the HA, local social services department and the local Community Health Council or other public/patient representative on the PCG Board

- others, such as pharmacists, can be co-opted onto the PCG Board
- specialist groups, such as prescribing committees, will operate below Board level
- accountability agreements between the HA and the PCG will set out targets, objectives and standards for the delivery of services, including medicines
- HAs and PCGs will be able to commission services through long-term agreements (i.e. three years plus) which will include commitment to NICE guidelines and NSFs
- PCGs will have incentives to provide cost-effective services
- selected PCGs will progress to Level 3 and 4 PCGs in 1999/2000
- all Level 3 and 4 PCGs will be fully independent PCTs in due course; all PCGs are expected to be PCTs within 10 years

Importance to the Pharmaceutical Industry

GPs will be more closely managed than they ever have been before. Level 1 and 2 PCGs will be tied to the HA. Despite the assurances that the right of clinical judgement by individual prescribers will be preserved, the Pharmaceutical Industry can expect the influence of HA prescribing advisers and formularies, as well as national formularies (i.e. Prodigy) to be strengthened.

In addition, PCG subgroups on prescribing will include at least one pharmacist. PCGs will have to sign up to NICE guidelines and NSFs as part of their accountability and service agreements.

HAs in consultation with Level 1 and 2 PCGs can commission services through longer term contracts than before. When in due course they become full PCTs, there may be scope for contracts for medicines in the way that contracts are currently negotiated with Acute Trusts.

Unified budgets

What's it all about?
Cash-limited unified budgets for HAs and PCGs will cover the cost of commissioning hospital and community health services, GP practice staff and premises and prescribing. The budgets aim for maximum flexibility in the way health care professionals use the resources available, by allowing funds to flow freely within the unified budget (e.g. both out of and into the prescribing part of the budget). For the first time all prescribing in the NHS will be cash-limited.

Key points
- unified budgets for HAs and Level 3 and 4 PCGs to cover the cost of commissioning hospital and community services, GP practice staff and premises and prescribing
- PCG budgets for Level 1 and 2 to cover staff and premises and prescribing only
- flexibility in allowing funds to flow from one element of the budget to the other as GPs see fit, but minimum levels set for spending on staff, premises and computers
- population basis for allocation to be based on GP list size after 1999/2000
- prescribing element of allocation weighted in favour of patients who are permanently sick, with no family or other carers, and infants and students; method of calculating prescribing element currently under review
- all parts of the budget, including prescribing, are cash-limited
- the way services are costed, the origin and quality of the data used and the assumptions underlying the estimates used by HAs and PCGs are to be transparent

Importance to the Pharmaceutical Industry
A formula is used to calculate the prescribing part of the unified budget. This may be helpful to pharmaceutical companies' marketing departments as it shows the assumptions made in calculating the resources available to HAs and PCGs for prescribing.

The primary aim of the unified budget (apart from tighter management through cash-limiting) is to maximise flexibility for PCGs to deploy resources to best meet the health needs of their patients. This means that funds can flow into, as well as out of, prescribing budgets. For this to happen, however, pharmaceutical companies will have to be able to demonstrate that their products provide value for money compared with alternative ways of using the resources. Pharmaceutical companies will also have to demonstrate that they are making a contribution to meeting national and local priorities for health and health care as set out in the local Health Improvement Programmes, for which PCGs will be expected to meet targets set through their accountability agreements with the HAs.

Prescribing incentives, rewards and risk assessment

What's it all about?
The introduction of cash-limited budgets for prescribing has led to the NHS Executive issuing guidance on incentives to encourage clinical and cost-effective prescribing. There will also be rewards for making savings in prescribing, assessing and managing the potential risks to the prescribing part of the unified budget each year.

Key points
- PCGs and GP practices will have an incentive scheme to encourage clinical and cost-effective prescribing
- savings achieved will be split equally between the PCG and the practice that achieves the saving
- the PCG's share of the savings will be used to fund any overspend amongst its practices
- savings can be used to fund initiatives to improve prescribing, but cannot be used to purchase medicines
- risk assessment and management will be used to assess the impact of fluctuations in prescribing, high cost medicines for small numbers of patients and new medicines on the annual cash-limited budgets

- HAs and PCGs will hold contingency reserves to cover perceived risks

Importance to the Pharmaceutical Industry

The guidance sets out the range of 'sticks and carrots' to be applied to prescribing in PCGs from April 1999. On one hand, practices and PCGs are to be offered shares in the savings achieved to develop a range of services within the practice. On the other hand, any savings accrued by the PCG must be used to off-set any over-prescribing by practices elsewhere in the PCG. Clearly, peer pressure is going to play a leading role in the management of medicines within PCGs.

A consequence of cash-limiting prescribing is that HAs/PCGs/practices will be using a risk assessment and management framework to ensure that, as far as possible, they stay within budget. How well they are able to do this will depend in part on the quality of information they receive from pharmaceutical companies. HAs and PCGs will have contingency reserves to bail out PCGs and practices where things go wrong. However, this could be damaging if such use of reserves is seen to be a result of unreliable information received from the pharmaceutical company concerned.

Information for health

What's it all about?

The new communications and information strategy for the NHS is an eight-year programme which underpins the policy objectives for the New NHS. It provides the means for the NHSE, GPs and other primary care professionals, HAs, Trusts, NICE and CHI to access information needed to carry out the tasks expected of them, including the management of the NHS Drugs Bill.

Key points

- there is to be a lifelong patient-based electronic health record, including a prescribing and dispensing record, which will be based in GP practice, but shared by all health care professionals in the NHS

- decision-support systems (e.g. the Prodigy prescribing system) to be developed for GPs, but only used in live clinical care after rigorous evaluation to the satisfaction of the professions
- all computerised GP practices to be connected to NHSnet by March 2000
- electronic links between GPs, community pharmacists and the Prescription Pricing Authority (PPA) for the exchange of prescription information
- no special computer systems for PCGs until specific information requirements have been fully worked out
- new National Electronic Library for Health holding NICE guidelines, CHI reports, R&D information, etc to be easily accessed by GPs via NHSnet and by the public via the Internet
- strategy to be partly funded from the £6bn Modernisation Fund for the NHS
- New NHS Information Authority to assume responsibility for NHS systems following the abolition of the NHSE's Information Management Group

Importance to the Pharmaceutical Industry

A key issue for the Government is how easily GPs and others in the NHS can access the range of advice and guidelines available to them, including those on prescribing and the use of medicines.

The new strategy, largely funded from the Modernisation Fund, aims to provide the means to do this by modernising primary care systems and linking them to the rest of the NHS. However, the emphasis at the moment remains at GP practice system development level. There are no immediate plans for specific PCG systems, although a working paper on PCG functional requirements is promised for 1999. This is likely to mean that formularies will be aimed at HAs or GP practices, rather than PCG-based.

The National Electronic Library for Health will be the main repository for NICE guidelines, CHI reports, Health Technology

Assessments and other research reports. All information held in the Library will be accredited. The criteria for accreditation are not yet known, but the Library is likely to be wary of information provided by pharmaceutical companies or sponsors. However, it may be possible to submit information as long as it is not seen as overtly promotional.

Prodigy is now freely available to all GP practices with computers (90% of all practices).

GP prescribing support

What's it all about?
The NHS Executive has published a resource pack and guide on prescribing support for GPs prepared by the NHS National Prescribing Centre (NPC), which will become part of NICE in Spring 1999. The guide brings together a range of models for, and experiences of, the effective management of prescribing as examples of best practice in the NHS.

Key points
- drug expenditure through GP prescribing in England amounts to £4.5 billion annually, representing about 50% of costs in primary care; prescribing costs are currently rising at 9% per annum
- emphasis on 'value for money' from medicines
- includes advice on using prescribing analyses, the development and use of guidelines and protocols, effective management of repeat prescribing, more generic prescribing, the use of computers in prescribing, better co-operation between Trusts and PCGs and the effective management of information on both old and new drugs
- sets out guidelines for the development of formularies at HA, PCG and practice level
- gives an example of a job description for a pharmacist advising a PCG on medicines

- states that GP computer systems have 'too many choices'
  of medicines for prescribing

Importance to the Pharmaceutical Industry

Despite references to clinical effectiveness, PCGs and the forthcoming collaboration with NICE, this document seems to suggest that the NPC maintains its narrow focus on the cost of medicines through prescribing in GP practice. There is little reference to the value of medicines in relation to other interventions, or to the cost consequences of failing to prescribe appropriately. For example, there is no attempt to relate the cost of prescribing to total health costs. The assertion that there are "too may prescribing choices" is astonishing and clearly linked to the Prodigy pilot trial prescribing computer system. It is a principle that is unlikely to be welcomed by the medical profession.

Nevertheless there are some useful pointers in the document relating to the future management of prescribing (e.g. the formulary development guidelines and the pharmacist adviser job description). It may provide the Pharmaceutical Industry with an opportunity to review its contact points with those who will have an impact on prescribing decision-making at all levels in the NHS and decide how best to meet the challenges of the 'new' NHS.

The Selected List of NHS Drugs

What's it all about?

The NHS Selected List was introduced into the NHS in 1985. Under the original list the prescribing of 17 categories of drugs was restricted to a limited list of cheap, mainly generic products. It was extended to include further categories in 1992. It has regained prominence by virtue of the Government's decision to use Schedule 11 of the list to restrict the prescribing of Viagra (sildenafil) and other male impotence medicines to specified categories of patient. This was seen as a precedent for future restrictions on prescribing of medicines to specified patients and/or conditions.

Key points

- the 17 therapeutic categories of restricted drugs are: analgesics for mild/moderate pain; antidiarrhoeals; appetite suppressants; benzodiazepines; contraceptives; cough/cold remedies; antiallergy drugs; drugs acting on the ear and nose; drugs acting on the skin; drugs for vaginal/vulval conditions; drugs used in anaemia; hypnotics and anxiolytics; indigestion remedies; laxatives; tonics; topical antirheumatics; and vitamins

- the Government proposes the inclusion of additional prescribing restrictions through Section 11 of the Selected List of NHS Drugs which has been previously been used to extend the list to meet an unmet clinical need (e.g. clobazam for epilepsy)

- the Government is aiming to keep expenditure on male impotency treatments within the current level of expenditure in the NHS (a 'nil cost' policy)

- savings elsewhere in the NHS Drugs Bill or within health and/or social service expenditure to off-set the cost of the medication may be valid, but such claims need to be supported by robust evidence

- the British Medical Association is opposed to restrictions, claiming that GPs should prescribe on the basis of clinical effectiveness rather than on cost grounds

- the Viagra issue may bring legal and ethical issues of cost containment vs clinical judgement to a head

Importance to the Pharmaceutical Industry

The proposed restrictions on Viagra and the other male impotency medications will set the precedent for how new medicines of significant potential cost to the NHS will be dealt with by the Government. As a starting point, the Government will be looking for a 'nil cost' solution. Pharmaceutical companies will need to consider the options for off-setting the cost to the NHS of such products, for example, within the Company's product portfolio, elsewhere in the NHS Drugs Bill, elsewhere within health and social services expenditure, etc. Any claims of savings must be supported by robust evidence.

The Pharmaceutical Price Regulation Scheme

What's it all about?

The Pharmaceutical Price Regulation Scheme (PPRS) is a voluntary agreement between the Government and the Association of the British Pharmaceutical Industry (APBI) relating to industry profits from sales of branded medicines to the NHS. The PPRS operates at the level of the individual pharmaceutical company and controls overall profits made by the company from its sales to the NHS rather than individual drug prices. It is currently under re-negotiation.

Key points

- it is a voluntary scheme
- concerned with profits from sales rather than individual drug prices
- covers branded products only (i.e. not unbranded generics)
- covers all pharmaceutical companies which sell to the NHS
- only those companies with sales over £20m per annum submit Annual Financial Returns (AFRs) as a basis for annual negotiation
- AFRs contain details of the total cost of sales to the NHS together with the relevant costs incurred (e.g. cost of cost of raw materials, manufacturing, distributing finished products)
- the most significant cost allowances are for research and development (R&D) and investment in the UK (e.g. factories)
- new products with expected sales of £20 million or more in any of the first five years on the market must be notified to the Department of Health
- PPRS agreements last 3-5 years before being re-negotiated
- the 1993 agreement included a 2.5% price reduction across the board for all companies
- the Government may use its statutory powers to fix prices if agreement with companies cannot be reached

Importance to the Pharmaceutical Industry

This scheme is of central importance to the Pharmaceutical Industry. The 1998 negotiations were set in the wider context of how the NHS Drugs Bill will be managed. Increased price sensitivity amongst prescribers (e.g. through cash-limited budgets) has raised doubts about the continuing need for PPRS.

Pharmaceutical companies need to decide whether or not to support PPRS. If they are in favour of the present scheme, they should consider what improvements could be made, if any. If they are against it, a viable alternative must be sought.

Management of medicines in the New NHS

What's it all about?

The Government views the effective management of medicines as a prime objective in the New NHS. Drug expenditure by GPs in England accounts for approximately £4.5 billion annually, representing about 50% of costs in primary care. Prescribing costs are currently rising at 9% per annum.

Management of medicines in the future will consist of a complex set of demand and supply side measures.

Key points

Measures include:

- *Pharmaceutical Pricing Regulation Scheme (PPRS)* – the 1993 agreement requires companies to notify the Department of Health if sales of a new medicine in any one year of the first five years after launch is expected to exceed £20 million. The Government also intends to add a statutory right to fix drug prices control profits from NHS sales if negotiations with pharmaceutical companies fail.
- *Selected List of NHS Drugs* – will be used to ban a medicine from NHS prescription (Schedule 10) or restrict its use to specified patients and/or conditions (Schedule 11).

- *NICE* – will provide guidelines and protocols for the NHS on clinical and cost-effectiveness. These will include guidelines and protocols on prescribing and the assessment of new medicines. It is expected that the National Prescribing Centre will continue to play a key role.
- *Horizon Scanning Unit* – based in Birmingham, aims to work with the Pharmaceutical Industry in identifying significant medicines at an early stage of development.
- *Prodigy* – supported by the NPC, Prodigy is a prescribing support computer system freely available to GPs. Prodigy limits recommended prescribing choice of medicines.
- *HA prescribing advisors* – likely to be key players given that PCGs (particularly Levels 1 and 2) are likely to come under pressure to adopt a HA-based formulary. They receive an analysis of prescribing in their area from the Prescription Pricing Authority. The prescribing of certain medicines will also feature in Health Improvement Programmes (e.g. for reducing teenage pregnancies).
- *PCG prescribing subgroups* – recommended in NHSE guidance on PCGs to manage the prescribing part of the unified budgets. The chairperson of each PCG needs to be identified.
- *Risk assessment and management* – shared between HAs, PCGs and GP practices. Need to ensure that they have the right information in order to make a realistic assessment.
- *Nurse prescribers* – likely to join GPs in prescribing in primary care practices.
- *Community pharmacists* – they may also become prescribers. Electronic links with GPs will allow a greater exchange of information on prescribing and dispensing. Pharmacists will also be giving advice to the PCG prescribing subcommittees on a part-time basis, although PCGs which achieve full Trust status may need a full-time appointment.
- *Trusts* – have their own formularies and are being encouraged to co-operate more closely with PCGs in the

development of joint protocols and guidelines for prescribing. Removal of budgetary barriers between Trust and PCGs should lead to prescribing across the interface.

- *NHS Supplies Authority* – will continue to supply medicines to Trusts with an emphasis on high volume/low cost products (e.g. generic medicines). Many Trusts now choose to 'go it alone' in negotiating prices. Likely to play a leading role in the Government's proposals for longer-term contracts for goods and services in the NHS (i.e. three years plus).

- *Commission for Health Improvement* – CHI will be using prescribing indicators as part of the National Framework for Assessing Performance of HAs and Trusts (and later PCGs). Their reports will be on specific Trusts and HAs and on selected 'themes' across the NHS.

- *National Prescribing Centre* – will continue to issue Medical Resource Centre reports. Pharmaceutical companies will need to ensure that they are accurate and fair. The NPC also runs seminars for HA prescribing advisers. Pharmaceutical companies will need to consider whether they can usefully contribute to these (e.g. on the launch of a new product).

Importance to the Pharmaceutical Industry

The Pharmaceutical Industry, along with other pharmaceutical companies, will need to consider how best to present itself and its products within the medicines management forum of the New NHS. Strategies are needed at national, regional and local level to identify key players in the NHS on prescribing issues and to make the Industry's products relevant to the agenda they are addressing.

The New NHS in Scotland, Wales and Northern Ireland

What's it all about?

When taking office in May 1997, the British government announced the launch of a programme of NHS reforms from April 1999. Although based on the same principles – national standards, local responsibility, partnership, efficiency, quality, and public confidence – the proposals for England, Scotland, Wales and Northern Ireland differed in several ways. The differences were inevitable, given the variety of infrastructures in the four countries and the imminent proposals for Scottish and Welsh devolution and the Good Friday Agreement in Northern Ireland.

Key points

- all proposals are based on the same six principles: national standards, local responsibility, partnership, efficiency, quality and public confidence
- proposals for England are based on HAs leading mandatory PCGs with cash-limited prescribing and other budgets; some PCGs will be able to commission services from Acute and Community Trusts, some will not
- proposals for Scotland are based on cash-limited budgets held by Health Boards which negotiate with Acute and Primary Care Trusts on services to be provided; GPs are grouped into voluntary Local Health Care Co-operatives GPs not in LHCCs manage a budget delegated by the PCT
- proposals for Wales are based on HAs holding cash-limited budgets with mandatory Local Health Groups to which GPs, pharmacists and other health professionals belong; LHCs commission services from Trusts on the basis of indicative budgets
- proposals for Northern Ireland are based on the existing joint management of health and social services by Health and Social Services Boards; GPs, pharmacists and other health professionals are accountable to HSSBs; Trusts provide both health and social services

- Scotland is the only country with tax raising powers (i.e. up to 3.5 pence in £)
- Northern Ireland is the only country that has made an explicit statement that all new medicines should be assessed for their clinical/cost-effectiveness before introduction into the NHS

Importance to the Pharmaceutical Industry

The Pharmaceutical Industry will have to review its arrangements for dealing with customers in each country and, in particular, will need to identify the key decision makers on prescribing.

At local level in England it is likely to be the HA prescribing advisers and the GPs who specialise in prescribing issues within the PCGs, plus the drug budget holders in the Trusts. In Scotland, it may be those who similarly specialise within the LHCCs or advisers within the Primary Care and Acute Trusts who are commissioned to provide the services or advisers in the HBs who hold the cash-limited budgets and commission the services. In Wales, it could be advisers in the HA which, at least initially, will hold the cash-limited budgets or the GPs who specialise in prescribing issues within the LHGs. In Northern Ireland, for the moment at least, it is the individual GP practice and Trust or advisers in the Health and Social Service Boards.

Local formularies, supported by national advice, may be found at any of these levels.

The New NHS: Questions for the Pharmaceutical Industry

Management Committee

1. What is our position on the Pharmaceutical Price Regulation Scheme (PPRS)? Are we a 'Return on Capital' (RoC) or 'Return on Sales' (RoS) company? Does this colour our view? If we support it, what changes would we like to see? If we do not support it, what alternatives would we like to see? What is our

view on the Government's intention to use statutory powers to fix drug prices or control profits from NHS sales in the event of failed negotiations?

2. What is our position on the Selected List of Drugs? Is Schedule 11 an acceptable way of controlling the availability of drugs on the NHS to certain patients and/or conditions? Is Schedule 10 preferable in some circumstances (because is enables some medicines to remain available to all)?

3. What is our position on the National Institute for Clinical Excellence (NICE)? Are we to be proactive (e.g. close co-operation to speed up assessments, participation in seminars for Health Authority prescribing advisers) or reactive (e.g. give the minimum required)? How can we ensure that NICE operates on a level playing field (i.e. not only with other medicines but with other forms of intervention)? What would happen if NICE fails? Can we afford to let this happen?

4. What is our position on the Horizon Scanning Unit? Are we to co-operate? If so how? What might the consequences be of not co-operating?

5. Would there be any value in seeing the Commission for Health Improvement (CHI) reports? Is so, how could this be done?

6. How can we best ensure that the patient representative groups we support get a fair hearing in the New NHS? At national level (i.e. the new National Forum)? At local level (e.g. Community Health Councils, discussions on the development of local HImPs, PCG/HA/ Trust Boards)?

7. What is our position on Prodigy? How can we ensure that our products get fair treatment? What can we do if our products are left out?

8. What opportunities does the Information for Health strategy present? Are there opportunities to donate information to the new Electronic Library for Health? Can we link our Company website to the Library? Can we communicate directly with GPs? What threats might the strategy pose?

9. Would there be any value in joining the discussions on the development of local HImPs in our role as a local employer/business? What would we learn about NHS planning at local level by doing so?

10. Would there be any value in participating in any of the Health Action Zones? What might we be able to contribute (e.g. money, expertise)? What might we gain from such participation? What might we lose?

11. Would there be any value in participating in the social exclusion initiatives (e.g. on reducing unwanted teenage pregnancies)? What might we able to contribute to the initiative? What might we gain from such participation? What might we lose?

12. Would there be any value in participating in the Healthy Schools Initiative? Are the local health/education authorities mounting any initiatives? What might we be able to contribute? What would gain from such participation? What might we lose?

13. What is our position on the Healthy Workplaces Initiative? What do we already do to encourage our employees to live a healthier lifestyle? Is there anything that that might be seen as embarrassing as a 'health service provider' (e.g. high level of absence through sickness)? Is there anything we could do to enhance the Company's image as a caring organisation?

14. Do we need separate strategies for Scotland, Wales and Northern Ireland?

Product Manager

1. What assessment process will be used by NICE? Will my products be assessed on an even playing field (i.e. on a clinical/cost-effectiveness basis in comparison with alternative interventions)?

2. Is anything to be gained by a better relationship with the National Prescribing Centre (e.g. by participating in seminars for HA prescribing advisors)?

3. What is the outcome of any relevant national initiatives?

4. What scope is there for including any of our products (or the therapeutic category in which they are included) in current or future National Service Frameworks?

5. Are there any Health Action Zones which may be relevant to my products?

6. Is the Healthy Schools Initiative a potential forum for educational material relevant to my products (e.g. the correct use of asthma inhalers)?

7. Are any of the Government's clinical effectiveness indicators of use to us (e.g. HRT vs hysterectomies for identifying HAs who are under-prescribing HRT)?

8. Is there anything we could usefully contribute on products or product-related health subjects to the New NHS Electronic Library for Health?

9. Will there be any Commission for Health Improvement reports on issues concerning the provision of health care across the NHS which are relevant to my products?

Sales Managers

1. Who is dealing with prescribing issues at the NHSE's regional offices?

2. Who are the HA prescribing advisors in my region?

3. How many of the HAs have formularies?

4. How many Primary Care Groups in my region are Levels 1 and 2? Are there any trials for Level 3 and 4 or Primary Care Trusts?

5. Are there any HAs within my region which have included local as well as national priorities, in the targets in their HiMPs which are relevant to our products?

6. What scope is there for long-term service agreements for the supply of medicines to Acute and Community Trusts?

7. What would be the impact on discounts to Trusts if there is prescribing across the interface between PCGs and Acute and Community Trusts and joint budgeting?

8. What do the Commission for Health Improvement reports say about the management of medicines in HAs and Trusts in my region?

Local Representatives

1. Who are the key decision-makers on prescribing in the PCGs in my area? Who are the members of the PCG prescribing subcommittee?

2. How tied are the PCGs to the HAs (i.e. are they Levels 1, 2, 3, 4 or a Trust)?

3. What scope might there be for long-term service agreements for the supply of medicines to Primary Care Trusts?

4. Are there a PCG formularies? Or are they using HA formularies? Have the GP practices got their own formulary? Different from PCG formularies?

5. Do the HAs/PCGs/practices have the appropriate information about our products to be able to make a realistic risk assessment of the impact of the products on their cash-limited budgets?

6. Have the PCGs employed pharmacist advisers? Will there be any benefit in talking to them about this role when I talk to them about dispensing and supply issues? Will I have to talk to them as prescribers?

7. Will I have to talk to nurses as well as GPs about prescribing?

8. Are they using a computer for generating prescriptions? Are they using the Prodigy system? Can they access information and advice about prescribing issues over NHSnet and/or the Internet?

Glossary

Accountability Agreements
Agreements between Health Authorities and Primary Care Groups on how the targets set in the local Health Improvement Programmes will be achieved, against which their performance will be assessed.

Clinical Freedom
The prescriber's right to prescribe what he or she sees as best for the patient. Still sacrosanct, but prescribers are under increasing pressure to conform with recommended prescribing guidelines and protocols.

Clinical Governance
A new statutory responsibility on all in the NHS for setting and meeting quality standards of care, including the appropriate and efficient use of medicines.

Clinical Effectiveness Indicators
One of a number of indicators used by the Commission for Health Improvement to assess performance in the NHS. Some indicators have either the reduction or increase in prescribing as a measure of success.

Clinical Outcomes Group
Main forum for representatives of the Department of Health/ NHS/professional colleges for co-ordinating the development of clinical guidelines. Likely to continue under the auspices of NICE.

Commission for Health Improvement
New statutory body set up to monitor the performance of Trusts, Health Authorities and Primary Care Groups in the NHS.

Department of Health
Whitehall department which is responsible for health and social services policy (e.g. *Our Healthier Nation*)

Electronic Library for Health
New on-line library containing advice on clinically effective treatment which will be open to those who work in the NHS (via NHSnet) and the public (via Internet).

A First Class Service
The Department of Health's consultative document on quality issues in the NHS, including clinical governance, NICE and the Commission for Health Improvement.

Formularies
Recommended lists of medicines to prescribe. May be formulated at national (Prodigy), Health Authority, PCG, practice or individual GP level.

Health Action Zones
Areas of particular deprivation which are given priority for resources in return for closer co-operation with the Health Authority, Local Authorities, local businesses and other local agencies in solving the problems.

Health Authorities
Responsible for health needs assessment for the local area and commissioning services from Trusts either with or on behalf of Primary Care Groups. New statutory responsibility to work jointly with Local Authorities on common issues.

Health Board
Health Authorities in Scotland.

Health Improvement Programmes
Local three-year plans for the health and well-being of the population in the local area. Developed by Health Authorities in consultation with local PCGs, Trusts, voluntary groups, representatives of the public and Local Authorities.

Health Resource Groups
The basis for costing services in the NHS (e.g. the National Schedule of Reference Costs). HRGs are a way of categorising the treatment received by patient. Each group contains a set of treatments ('treatment episodes') that are clinically similar and use roughly the same level of resources.

Health Services Directorate
Part of the NHS Executive. Responsible for medical and clinical effectiveness issues.

Health and Social Services Boards
Responsible for the joint management of health and social services in Northern Ireland.

Healthy Initiatives
Government initiatives to improve health, thus preventing avoidable illness. They include Healthy Neighbourhoods (aimed at improving the environment for the elderly), Healthy Schools and Healthy Workplaces.

Horizon Scanning
'Horizon scanning' is identifying new interventions and products under development at the earliest possible stage and well before they become available for general use in the NHS. It is the responsibility of the Horizon Scanning Unit at Birmingham University.

Incentives
Incentives to GPs and other prescribers to prescribe medicines which are clinically and cost-effective. Linked to rewards for doing so (i.e. 50/50 split on the consequent savings between the Primary Care Groups and the practice that made the savings). Savings can be used to improve services to patients.

Information for Health
The information strategy for the NHS which includes proposals for electronic prescribing and an Electronic Library for Health.

Local Authorities
Local government authorities responsible for social services as well as housing, the environment, education, etc. Have a statutory responsibility to work with Health Authorities in meeting the health and well-being need of the local population.

Local Health Care Co-operatives
Voluntary groups of GPs in Scotland who report to Primary Care Trusts.

Local Health Groups
Groups of GPs, pharmacists and other health professionals in Wales. Membership is mandatory.

Our Healthier Nation
The Government's Green Paper setting out the national targets for health.

National Forum
New forum for representatives of patients and carers to input on health and social care policy at national level.

National Framework for Assessing Performance
Framework of performance indicators used by the Commission for Health Improvement to measure the quality of services provided in the NHS.

National Institute for Clinical Excellence
New body set up to make clinical effectiveness recommendations on new health interventions, including medicines. Recommendations within National Service Frameworks are expected to be complied with.

National Prescribing Centre
Now absorbed into NICE, but expected to continue to play a leading role on the evaluation of new medicines and other prescribing issues.

National Schedule of Reference Costs

Schedule of average costs of treatment in Trusts which enables comparisons with other Trusts, Health Authorities and PCGs when negotiating service agreements with Trusts.

National Service Frameworks

Sets of national clinical guidelines, protocols and service configuration on priority areas which the NHS is expected to follow. Includes NICE guidelines on prescribing.

National Survey of Patient and User Experience

Annual surveys of patients and carers on the quality of the service they receive from the NHS.

The New NHS: Modern, Dependable

The Government's White Paper on changes to the organisation and operation of the NHS from April 1999.

NHS Bill 1999

Parliamentary bill which, if passed, will establish Primary Care Trusts and the Commission for Health Improvement, and will also give the Government reserve powers to fix drug prices in the NHS and control pharmaceutical company profits.

NHS Executive

Part of the Department of Health, the NHSE is the headquarters of the NHS and is responsible for operational policy (e.g. prescribing and dispensing).

NHSnet

The NHS computer network system that will allow users to exchange records and mail and access databases to gain advice on clinically effective treatments and other guidance.

Pharmaceutical Price Regulation Scheme

The Pharmaceutical Price Regulation Scheme (PPRS) is a voluntary agreement between the Government and the Association of the

British Pharmaceutical Industry (APBI) on the profits the Industry makes from sales of branded medicines to the NHS.

Planning and Priorities Guidance
Issued each year by the NHS Executive as guidance on priorities in the NHS for the forthcoming year. In 1998, for the first time, it provided joint health and social services guidance and covered a period of three years.

Primary Care Groups
Groups of around 50 GPs, nurses and other health professionals responsible for providing primary care services around 100,000 patients. The are four types: advisory committee to the HA (Level 1); subcommittee of HA with a devolved budget (Level 2); stand-alone body able to commission health services from Trust (Level 3); and stand-alone body able to commission full range of health and social services (Level 4).

Prodigy
Prodigy is a decision support computer system which aims to improve the effectiveness (both quality and cost) of GP prescribing.

Risk Assessment
Framework to enable HAs, PCG and GP practices to assess prescribing risks and to manage the subsequent risk effectively, without overspending. Prescribing risks include seasonal and other fluctuations, newly introduced medicines, and prescribing high cost medicines to small numbers of patients.

Selected List of Drugs
Scheme which enables the Government to control the availability of certain categories of drugs on the NHS. Schedule 10 drugs are those on which there is a total ban from prescribing on the NHS (although suitable alternatives exist). Schedule 11 drugs are available only for specified patients and/or conditions.

Service Agreements

Three-year agreements between HAs/PCGs and Trusts for the provision of services in line with the objectives of the local Health Improvement Programme. May include the use of agreed unified primary/secondary care guidelines and protocols, including those for medicines.

Social Exclusion

Social exclusion is a shorthand label for what can happen when individuals or areas suffer from a combination of linked problems such as unemployment, poor skills, low incomes, poor housing, high crime environments, bad health and family breakdown.

Social Exclusion Unit

The Social Exclusion Unit, based at the Cabinet Office, takes the lead on long-term issues of social deprivation which cross the boundaries of two or more Government departments' remits.

Trusts

Self-managed providers of health care consisting of Acute Trusts (providing hospital services), Community Trusts (providing community health services) and Mental Health Trusts (providing the full range of hospital and community health services). All PCGs are expected to become Primary Health Care Trusts in due course.

Unified Budgets

Budgets allocated by Health Authorities to Primary Care Groups. Unlike previous budgets, funds can flow from one part of the budget to another according to where they can be most effectively used, and are cash-limited.

Selected Bibliography

Audit Commission

1   Dear to Our Hearts? Commissioning Services for the Treatment and Prevention of CHD (1995)

2   Goods For Your Health: Improving Supplies Management in the NHS Trusts (1997)

3   Higher Purchase: Commissioning Specialised Services in the NHS (1997)

Government Papers

Parliamentary Bill

4   Health Bill 14HL-EN (House of Lords, 1999)

White Papers

5   Designed to Care: Renewing the National Health Service in Scotland (Scottish Office, 1997)

6   NHS Wales: Putting Patients First (Welsh Office, 1998)

7   Scotland's Parliament (Scottish Office, 1997)

8   A Mayor and Assembly for London: The Government's proposals for Modernising the Governance of London (Department of the Environment, Transport & The Regions, 1998)

9   The New NHS Modern, Dependable (Department of Health, 1997)

10   Voice For Wales (Welsh Office, 1997)

11   Well Into 2000 (Northern Ireland Office, 1998)

12   Your Right To Know: Freedom of Information (Office of the Chancellor of the Duchy of Lancaster, 1997)

Green Paper

13   Our Healthier Nation: A Contract for Health (Department of Health, 1998)

Agreement

14   The Good Friday Agreement (UK/Eire Governments, 1998)

Other Government Documents

15   A First Class Service: Quality in the New NHS (Department of Health, 1998)

16   A National Framework for Assessing Performance: Consultation Document (NHS Executive, 1998)

17   A Policy Framework for Commissioning Cancer Services: A Report by the Expert Advisory Group on Cancer to the Chief Medical Officers of England and Wales (Department of Health/Welsh Office, 1995)

18   An Interim Report of a Project to Strengthen the Public Health Function in England (Department of Health, 1998)

19   Clinical Audit in the NHS (NHS Executive, 1996)

20   Clinical Effectiveness Indicators: A Consultation Document (NHS Executive, 1998)

21   Clinical Guidelines: Using Clinical Guidelines to Improve Patient Care Within the NHS

22   Crown Interim Report: Review of Prescribing, Supply and Administration of Medicines: A Report on The Supply and Administration of Medicines Under Group Protocols (Department of Health, 1998)

23   GP Prescribing Support: A Resource Document and Guide for the New NHS (National Prescribing Centre/NHS Executive, 1998)

24   Information for Health: An Information Strategy for the Modern NHS 1998-2005 (NHS Executive, 1998)

25   Modernising Mental Health Services: Safe, Sound and Supportive (Department of Health, 1998)

26   A National Framework for Assessing Performance (NHS Executive, 1998)

27   Partnership in Action (Department of Health, 1998)

28   Pharmaceutical Price Regulation Scheme (Department of Health/Association of British Pharmaceutical Industry, 1993)

29   Prodigy Interim Report (The Sowerby Unit for Primary Care Informatics, 1996)

30   R&D: Towards an Evidence-based Health Service (Department of Health, 1995)

31   The New NHS: 1998 Reference Costs (NHS Executive, 1998)

32   Your NHS - A Force For Health (Department of Health, 1998)

NHS Executive Circulars
33   Executive Letter EL(94)72: Purchasing and Prescribing

34   Executive Letter EL(95)97: New Drugs for Multiple Sclerosis

35   Executive Letter EL(96)17: The Operation of Community Health Councils from April 1996

36   Executive Letter EL(97)65: Health Action Zones: Invitation to Bid

37   Health Service Circular HSC1998/021: Better Health and Better Health Care

38   Health Service Circular HSC 1998/055: National Schedule of Reference Costs: Data Collection

39   Health Service Circular HSC 1998/065: Establishing Primary Care Groups

40   Health Service Circular HSC 1998/074: National Service Frameworks

41   Health Service Circular HSC 1998/120: Setting Unified Health Authority and Primary Care Group Budgets

42   Health Service Circular HSC1998/121: Better Health and Better Health Care: The Next Steps

43   Health Service Circular HSC 1998/139: Developing PCGs

44   Health Service Circular HSC 1998/159: Modernising Health and Social Services: National Priorities Guidance 1999/00-2001/02

45   Health Service Circular HSC 1998/167: Health Improvement Programmes: Better Planning for Health and Better Health Care

46   Health Service Circular HSC 1998/171: Guidance on Health Authority and Primary Care Group Allocations

47   Health Service Circular HSC 1998/198: Commissioning in the New NHS: Commissioning Services 1999-2000

48   Health Service Circular HSC 1998/218: National Service Framework for Coronary Heart Disease: Emerging Findings Report

49   Health Service Circular HSC 1998/228: The New NHS Modern and Dependable: Primary Care Groups: Delivering the Agenda

50   Health Service Circular HSC 1998/230: The New NHS Modern and Dependable: Governing Arrangements for Primary Care Groups

51   Health Circular HSC 1998/232: Nurse Prescribing: Implementing the Scheme Across England

52   Health Circular HSC 1998/233: Modernising Mental Health Services: Safe, Sound and Supportive

Brookwood Medical Publications Ltd publishes a range of handbooks and reports on clinical research and regulatory affairs for the global pharmaceutical industry.

For further details contact Garrett Murphy on +44 (0)181 332 4600 (tel), +44 (0)181 332 4610 (fax) or e-mail joanna@bwedit.demon.co.uk.